THE WAY OF THE

A Pathway to Life Everlasting

James Mulligan

Published 2015 by Boanerges Press

ISBN-13: 978-1506195827

ISBN-10: 1506195822

Prayer meditations

by

Saint Francis of Assisi

Blessed John Henry Newman

Cover illustration
ECCE HOMO   Lithograph by Otto Dix

History of the Way of the Cross in Church devotional practice

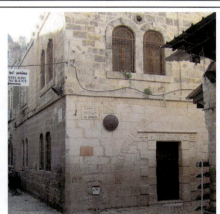

Via Dolorosa: 5th Station

And as they came out, they found a man of Cyrene, Simon by name: him they compelled to bear his cross.

Matthew 27

**Jerusalem
Via Dolorosa**

The *Way of the Cross* is a devotion that recalls in very evocative fashion the last hours of Jesus in his earthly life: from when he and his disciples, after psalms had been sung, left for the Mount of Olives, until the Lord was crucified at Golgotha (Place of The Skull) and buried in a garden nearby in a new tomb hewn out of rock.

The Church has from the earliest kept alive the words and the events of the painful path Jesus walked from the Mount of Olives to the Mount of Calvary.

Archaeological findings prove the existence of, as early as the second century, expressions of pious worship at the tomb near Calvary. At the end of the fourth century a pilgrim lady named Aetheria tells us in *Peregrinatio Etheriae* (Discovered in 1884 in an 11th-century Latin manuscript at Arezzo, Italy.) of three holy buildings on the hill of Golgotha: the *Anastasis*, the little church *ad Crucem*, and the great church – the *Martyrium*. Aetheria describes a procession from the *Anastasis* to the *Martyrium* which took place on certain days. This was not a *Way of the Cross*, but that procession, with its chanting of psalms and close connection with the places of the Passion, is considered by some scholars an embryonic form of the future *Way of the Cross*.

The *Way of the Cross* with its fourteen stations as we have the devotion today dates to the late Middle Ages. Saint Bernard of Clairvaux (+ 1153), Saint Francis of Assisi (+ 1226) and Saint Bonaventure of Bagnoregio (+ 1274), with their loving, contemplative devotion, prepared the ground on which the devout practice was to develop.

The traditional form of the Stations of the Cross

The *Way of the Cross* or *Via Crucis*, in its present form, is recorded in Spain in the first half of the seventeenth century especially in Franciscan communities. From the Iberian Peninsula it spread first to Sardinia, at that time under the dominion of the Spanish crown and then to Italy. Here it found a most assiduous apostle in Saint Leonard of Port Maurice (+ 1751), a Franciscan Friar and a tireless missionary, he personally erected more than 572 *Via Crucis*, including the famous one erected inside the Coliseum in Rome at the request of Benedict XIV.

Saint Leonard of Port Maurice

The biblical form of the Stations of the Cross

The biblical *Way of the Cross* omits stations which lack precise biblical reference such as the Lord's three falls (III, V, VII), Jesus' encounter with his Mother (IV) and with Veronica (VI). Instead we have stations such as Jesus' agony in the Garden of Olives (I), the unjust sentence passed by Pilate (V), the promise of paradise to the Good Thief (XI), the presence of the Mother and the Disciple at the foot of the Cross (XIII). Clearly these episodes are of great salvific import and theological significance for the drama of Christ's passion: an ever-present drama in which every man and woman, knowingly or unknowingly, plays a part.

The passion and death of Jesus in art

The passion and the death of Jesus, and later the Stations the Cross, have long been fruitful subjects for the work of artists. We have a rich catalogue of splendid and varied depictions of the last hours of Christ on earth from the work of such artist as Fra Angelico, Duccio, Titian, Rembrandt through to the twentieth century expressionist work of Emile Nolde, Lovis Corinth, Otto Dix and to modern day painters such as Peter Howson.

The Crucifixion   Emile Nolde

Christ Mocked — Otto Dix

The Veil of Veronica (c. 1618-1622)

Domenico Fetti

Jesus Is Taken Down From The Cross

Rembrandt van Rijn

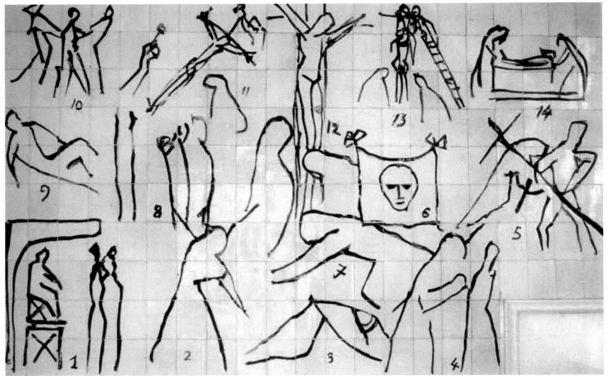
Stations of the Cross in the Chapel of Rosary at the Dominican Convent in Vence

One of the best known and indeed most admired modern day depictions of the Stations of the Cross was completed in April 1949 by the French artist Henri Matisse for the Chapel of the Rosary at the convent of Dominican nuns in Vence in the south of France.

Matisse, on a white-tiled ceramic panel, 13ft in length and 6½ft high, has painted a mural to be 'read' from the bottom left corner, snaking around over three rows, with the fourteen scenes arranged together like a puzzle. Indeed, the fourteen stations are not arranged in neat squares or patterns but instead almost overlap each other, cutting out of their rows and into the scenes below and above their own. Despite being in chronological order and arranged in rows, The Stations of the Cross are thus not primarily 'read' individually but instead absorbed as a comprehensive, united scene of Christ' suffering. It seems that it is the drama of the story, not the events of the crucifixion, that Matisse intended to depict, and to this end, the distillation of the lines and forms of the figures advances the emotive intensity of the scene.

Prayer Meditations

The prayer meditations in this book are by Saint Francis of Assisi and by Blessed John Henry Newman. The Way of the Cross has always produced meditations of outstanding quality. St Francis' and Blessed John Henry Newman's are among the most penetrating and enduring.

St Francis of Assisi

St Francis was born Giovanni di Bernardone around 1181 in Assisi, duchy of Spoleto, Italy. In his infancy his father, Pietro, began calling him Francesco. His father was a wealthy cloth merchant who owned farmland around Assisi. His mother was French. Francis wanted for nothing during his youth. He was in fact thoroughly spoiled and by the time he became a teenager he had developed into a tearaway who frequently drank, partied and broke the city curfew. He was also known for his charm and for being dandy in his dress.

At the age of twenty or thereabouts, during a petty war between the towns of Assisi and Perugia, he was taken prisoner. During a year of captivity, despite the hardships in wretched confinement, he remained cheerful and kept up the spirits of his companions. Soon after his release he suffered a long illness. After his recovery Francis joined another war-bound expedition from Assisi but on the first day fell ill. While lying helpless, a voice seemed to tell him to turn back, and "serve the Master rather than the man." Francis obeyed. At home he began to take long rambles in the country and to spend many hours by himself; he felt contempt for a life wasted on trivial and transitory things. Riding on horseback one day in the plains below Assisi he met a leper whose loathsome sores filled Francis with horror. Overcoming his revulsion he leapt from his horse and pressed into the leper's hand all the money he had with him, then kissed the hand. This was a turning point in his life. He started visiting the makeshift hospitals of the region, especially a refuge for lepers, which most persons avoided. On a pilgrimage to Rome he emptied his purse at St. Peter's tomb, then went out to the swarm of beggars at the door, gave his clothes to the one that looked poorest, dressed himself in this pauper's rags, and stood there all day with hand outstretched. The rich young man would experience for himself the humility of poverty.

One day, after his return from Rome, as he prayed in the humble little church of San Damiano outside the walls of Assisi, he felt the eyes of the Christ on the crucifix gazing at him and heard a voice saying three times, "Francis, go and repair My house, which you see is falling down." Taking this behest literally as referring to the church of San Damiano Francis went to his father's shop, impulsively bundled together a load of coloured drapery, and mounting his horse hastened to the nearby town of Foligno to a market of some importance and there sold both horse and drapery to procure the money needed for the restoration of the San Damiano church. His father Pietro was incensed at his son's conduct and the fearful Francis hid himself in a cave near San Damiano for a whole month. When he returned to the town, emaciated with hunger, Francis was followed by a hooting rabble, pelted with mud and stones, and mocked as a madman. He was dragged home by his father, beaten, bound, and locked in a dark closet.

Freed by his mother during Pietro Bernardone's absence, Francis returned at once to San Damiano where he found a shelter with the officiating priest. Francis took to wearing a coarse sackcloth tunic, something then worn by the poorest Umbrian peasants, and tied it round him with a knotted rope. He prayed fervently and openly exhorting the people of the countryside to the Gospel values of contrition, forgiveness, penance, brotherly love and peace.

The people of Assisi in time ceased to scoff at Francis. They now paused in wonderment; his example even drew others to him. Bernard of Quintavalle, a magnate of the town, was the first to join Francis, and he was soon followed by Peter of Cattaneo, a well-known canon of the cathedral. He began to attract more followers, and in 1209 with the papal blessing he founded the Friars Minor (Franciscans). Then in 1212, with St. Clare of Assisi, he founded the 'Poor Clares'. He also founded the 'Third Order of Penance' (the Third Order Franciscans) which included lay people. He took to a life of preaching and constant prayer. He displayed a great love of all of God's creation – birds, animals, nature and the seasons in all their manifestations. On or about the feast of the Exaltation of the Cross (14th September 1224), while praying on the mountainside there appeared on his body the visible marks of the five wounds (Stigmata) of the Crucified Christ. He was the first person in Church history known to have received the Stigmata.

St Francis died on October 3rd 1226. He was canonized in 1228 by Pope Gregory IX.

Patron: *against fire; animals; Catholic Action; dying alone; ecology; environment; families; fire; lace makers; merchants; peace; zoos; Italy; Assisi, Italy; Colorado; Sante Fe, New Mexico; archdiocese of San Francisco, California; archdiocese of Denver, Colorado; New Mexico; diocese of Salina; Kansas..*

Symbols: *birds and animals; bag of gold and rich raiment at his feet; winged crucifix with five rays; stigmata; crown of thorns; lighted lamp; fiery chariot; birds; deer; fish; skull; wolf; fire.*

Saint Francis of Assisi in Prayer ... Caravaggio

Saint Francis Receives The Stigmata

Lodovico Cardi

The patched habit worn by Saint Francis of Assisi preserved in the St Francis Museum in Assisi

St Francis by Cimabue

Blessed John Henry Newman

John Henry Newman began his career as an Anglican churchman and scholar and ended it as a Roman Catholic cardinal.

John Henry Newman was born in London on 21st February 1801, the eldest of six children of London banker. He grew up in the Church of England. As a teenager he experienced a deep religious conversion and resolved to spend the rest of his life in the pursuit of holiness.

In 1822 he was elected a fellow of Oriel College, Oxford, was ordained as an Anglican priest in 1825, and in 1828 became the Vicar of the University church of St Mary's. He became a leading light in the Oxford Movement, seeking to recover elements of catholicity within Anglicanism. In 1843 he resigned his living at St Mary's and retired to a converted stable block at Littlemore just outside Oxford, to think and pray. He was joined there by a number of his young followers and together they lived an austere semi-monastic life. Late in the evening on 8th October 1845, an Italian priest, Father Dominic Barberi (now Blessed), came to Littlemore. For several hours he heard Newman's first confession, and the next day he was received into the Catholic Church. In 1846 Newman went to Rome to study for the priesthood and was ordained priest there on Trinity Sunday 1847, at the age of forty six. He then returned to England and the English Oratory was founded in February 1848 in Birmingham. Meanwhile Father Wilfrid Faber had also converted from Anglicanism and he and several other converts joined Newman's new Oratory. Faber was then sent to establish the Oratory in London in May 1849.

Newman was always a prolific writer of letters, sermons and articles, and this continued throughout his life. His work was sometimes misunderstood, and a number of projects that he was asked to lead or support seemed to come to nothing. At one stage he was even wrongly suspected of doctrinal unorthodoxy. At times he must have felt that he was living under a cloud of disapproval. In 1879 the cloud was lifted. At the age of seventy eight he was made a Cardinal of the Holy Roman Church by Pope Leo XIII. Newman chose as his cardinalatial motto the words "Cor ad cor loquitur" (heart speaks to heart). He lived out the rest of his days, quietly and prayerfully, and still writing, at the Birmingham Oratory. He was taken to his eternal reward on 11th August 1890. His funeral procession from the Birmingham Oratory to Rednal attracted crowds of 15-20,000 onlookers, and he was lauded in the national press both in England and abroad.

In 1958 the cause for his canonisation was opened. In 1991 the Vatican's Congregation for the Causes of Saints declared that John Henry Newman had practiced the virtues to an heroic degree and he was proclaimed 'Venerable'. In October 2005 the postulator of the cause announced a potential miracle; Jack Sullivan, a Catholic deacon in Massachusetts, USA, attributed his recovery from a crippling spinal cord disorder to Newman's intercession in heaven.

On 3rd July 2009 His Holiness Pope Benedict XVI approved the authenticity of the miracle, thus opening the way for Newman's beatification. Beatification is the solemn affirmation by the Church that the servant of God may rightly be counted as being among the ranks of the Blessed, and that his prayers in heaven may laudably be sought by the faithful on earth.

The Holy Father, Pope Benedict XVI, beatified Cardinal Newman on September 19th, 2010 in Birmingham, during His State Visit to Great Britain.

Information above on the life of Blessed John Henry Newman courtesy the London Oratory

Act of Contrition

O my God I stand here sinful and sorrowful. I ask you to come to my aid. I never wish to fall into sin again.

First Station ... Jesus is condemned to death

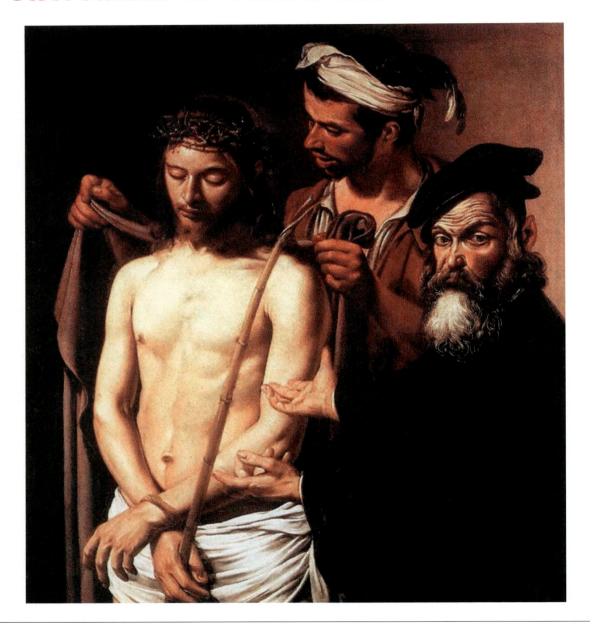

A Reading from the Holy Gospel according to Mark 14: 43-46

While Jesus was still speaking, Judas, one of the Twelve, arrived, accompanied by a crowd with swords and clubs, who had come from the chief priests, the scribes, and the elders. His betrayer had arranged a signal with them, saying, "the man I shall kiss is the one; arrest him and lead him away securely." He came and immediately went over to him and said, "Rabbi." And he kissed him. At this they laid hands on him and arrested him.

A Reading from the Holy Gospel according to Luke 22: 66-71

When day came the council of elders of the people met, both chief priests and scribes, and they brought him before their Sanhedrin. They said, "If you are the Messiah, tell us," but he replied to them, "If I tell you, you will not believe, and if I question, you will not respond. But from this time on the Son of Man will be seated at the right hand of the power of God." They all asked, "Are you then the Son of God?" He replied to them, "You say that I am." Then they said, "What further need have we for testimony? We have heard it from his own mouth."

A Reading from the Holy Gospel according to Mark 15:12-13, 15

Pilate again said to them, "Then what shall I do with the man whom you call the King of the Jews?" And they cried out again, "Crucify him." Pilate, wishing to satisfy the crowd, released for them Barabbas; and having scourged Jesus, he delivered him to be crucified.

We adore you O Christ, and we praise you.

Because by your Holy Cross you have redeemed the world.

A Prayer Meditation by Saint Francis of Assisi

Jesus, most innocent, who neither did nor could commit a sin, was condemned to death, and moreover, to the most ignominious death of the cross. To remain a friend of Caesar, Pilate delivered Him into the hands of His enemies. A fearful crime - to condemn Innocence to death, and to offend God in order not to displease men!

O innocent Jesus, having sinned, I am guilty of eternal death, but Thou willingly dost accept the unjust sentence of death, that I might live. For whom, then, shall I henceforth live, if not for Thee, my Lord? Should I desire to please men, I could not be Thy servant. Let me, therefore, rather displease men and all the world, than not please Thee, O Jesus.

A Prayer Meditation by Blessed John Henry Newman

THE Holy, Just, and True was judged by sinners, and put to death. Yet, while they judged, they were compelled to acquit Him. Judas, who betrayed Him, said, "I have sinned in that I have betrayed the innocent blood." Pilate, who sentenced Him, said, "I am innocent of the blood of this just person," and threw the guilt upon the Jews. The Centurion who saw Him crucified said, "Indeed this was a just man." Thus ever, O Lord, Thou art justified in Thy words, and dost overcome when Thou art judged. And so, much more, at the last day "They shall look on Him whom they pierced"; and He who was condemned in weakness shall judge the world in power, and even those who are condemned will confess their judgment is just.

Our Father
Hail Mary
Glory Be

Lord Jesus, crucified, have mercy on us!

STABAT MATER

At the cross her station keeping,
Stood the mournful Mother weeping,
Close to Jesus to the last.

Second Station ... Jesus carries his cross

A Reading from the Holy Gospel according to Mark 15:20

When they had mocked him, they stripped him of the purple cloak, and put his own clothes on him. And they led him out to crucify him.

We adore you O Christ, and we praise you.

Because by your Holy Cross you have redeemed the world.

A Prayer Meditation by Saint Francis of Assisi

When our divine Savior beheld the cross, He most willingly stretched out His bleeding arms, lovingly embraced it, and tenderly kissed it, and placing it on His bruised shoulders, He, although almost exhausted, joyfully carried it.

O my Jesus, I cannot be Thy friend and follower, if I refuse to carry the cross. O dearly beloved cross! I embrace thee, I kiss thee, I joyfully accept thee from the hands of my God. Far be it from me to glory in anything, save in the cross of my Lord and Redeemer. By it the world shall be crucified to me and I to the world, that I may be Thine forever.

A Prayer Meditation by Blessed John Henry Newman

JESUS supports the whole world by His divine power, for He is God; but the weight was less heavy than was the Cross which our sins hewed out for Him. Our sins cost Him this humiliation. He had to take on Him our nature, and to appear among us as a man, and to offer up for us a great sacrifice. He had to pass a life in penance, and to endure His passion and death at the end of it. O Lord God Almighty, who dost bear the weight of the whole world without weariness, who bore the weight of all our sins, though they wearied Thee, as Thou art the Preserver of our bodies by Thy Providence, so be Thou the Saviour of our souls by Thy precious blood.

Our Father
Hail Mary
Glory Be

Lord Jesus, crucified, have mercy on us!

STABAT MATER

Through her heart, His sorrow sharing
All His bitter anguish bearing,
Now at length the sword has passed.

Third Station ... Jesus falls the first time

A Reading from the Prophet Isaiah 53:5

He was wounded for our transgressions, he was bruised for our iniquities; upon him was the chastisement that made us whole, and with his stripes we are healed.

A reading from the Gospel according to Matthew 11:28-30

"Come to me, all who labour and are heavy laden, and I will give you rest. Take my yoke upon you, and learn from me; for I am gentle and lowly in heart, and you will find rest for your souls. For my yoke is easy, and my burden is light".

We adore you O Christ, and we praise you.

Because by your Holy Cross you have redeemed the world.

A Prayer Meditation by Saint Francis of Assisi

Our dear Saviour, carrying the cross, was so weakened by its heavy weight as to fall exhausted to the ground. Our sins and misdeeds were the heavy burden which oppressed Him: the cross was to Him light and sweet, but our sins were galling and insupportable.

O my Jesus, Thou didst bear my burden and the heavy weight of my sins. Should I, then, not bear in union with Thee, my easy burden of suffering and accept the sweet yoke of Thy commandments? Thy yoke is sweet and Thy burden is light: I therefore willingly accept it. I will take up my cross and follow Thee.

A Prayer Meditation by Blessed John Henry Newman

SATAN fell from heaven in the beginning; by the just sentence of his Creator he fell, against whom he had rebelled. And when he had succeeded in gaining man to join him in his rebellion, and his Maker came to save him, then his brief hour of triumph came, and he made the most of it. When the Holiest had taken flesh, and was in his power, then in his revenge and malice he determined, as he himself had been struck down by the Almighty arm, to strike in turn a heavy blow at Him who struck him. Therefore it was that Jesus fell down so suddenly. O dear Lord, by this Thy first fall raise us all out of sin, who have so miserably fallen under its power.

Our Father
Hail Mary
Glory Be

Lord Jesus, crucified, have mercy on us!

STABAT MATER

O, how sad and sore distressed
Was that Mother highly blessed
Of the sole-begotten One!

Fourth Station ... Jesus meets his afflicted mother

A Reading from the Holy Gospel according to Luke 2:34-35, 51

Simeon blessed them and said to Mary his mother, "Behold, this child is set for the fall and rising of many in Israel, and for a sign that is spoken against (and a sword will pierce through your own soul also), that thoughts out of many hearts may be revealed." His mother kept all these things in her heart.

We adore you O Christ, and we praise you.

Because by your Holy Cross you have redeemed the world.

A Prayer Meditation by Saint Francis of Assisi

How painful and how sad it must have been for Mary, the sorrowful Mother, to behold her beloved Son, laden with the burden of the cross! What unspeakable pangs her most tender heart experienced! How earnestly did she desire to die in place of Jesus, or at least with Him! Implore this sorrowful Mother that she assist you in the hour of your death.

O Jesus, O Mary, I am the cause of the great and manifold pains which pierce your loving hearts! Oh, that also my heart would feel and experience at least some of your sufferings! O Mother of Sorrows, let me participate in the sufferings which thou and Thy Son endured for me, and let me experience thy sorrow, that afflicted with thee, I may enjoy thy assistance in the hour of my death.

A Prayer Meditation by Blessed John Henry Newman

THERE is no part of the history of Jesus but Mary has her part in it. There are those who profess to be His servants, who think that her work was ended when she bore Him, and after that she had nothing to do but disappear and be forgotten. But we, O Lord, Thy children of the Catholic Church, do not so think of Thy Mother. She brought the tender infant into the Temple, she lifted Him up in her arms when the wise men came to adore Him. She fled with Him to Egypt, she took Him up to Jerusalem when He was twelve years old. He lived with her at Nazareth for thirty years. She was with Him at the marriage-feast. Even when He had left her to preach, she hovered about Him. And now she shows herself as He toils along the Sacred Way with His cross on His shoulders. Sweet Mother, let us ever think of thee when we think of Jesus, and when we pray to Him, ever aid us by thy powerful intercession.

Our Father
Hail Mary
Glory Be

Lord Jesus, crucified, have mercy on us!

STABAT MATER

Christ above in torment hangs,
She beneath beholds the pangs,
Of her dying, glorious Son.

Fifth Station... Simon of Cyrene helps Jesus carry his cross

A reading from the Gospel according to Luke 23:26

And as they led Jesus away, they seized one Simon of Cyrene, who was coming in from the country, and laid on him the cross, to carry it behind Jesus.

We adore you O Christ, and we praise you.

Because by your Holy Cross you have redeemed the world.

A Prayer Meditation by Saint Francis of Assisi

Simon of Cyrene was compelled to help Jesus carry His cross, and Jesus accepted his assistance. How willingly would He also permit you to carry the cross: He calls, but you hear Him not; He invites you, but you decline. What a reproach, to bear the cross reluctantly!

O Jesus! Whosoever does not take up his cross and follow Thee, is not worthy of Thee. Behold, I join Thee in the Way of Thy Cross; I will be Thy assistant, following Thy bloody footsteps

A Prayer Meditation by Blessed John Henry Newman

JESUS could bear His Cross alone, did He so will; but He permits Simon to help Him, in order to remind us that we must take part in His sufferings, and have a fellowship in His work. His merit is infinite, yet He condescends to let His people add their merit to it. The sanctity of the Blessed Virgin, the blood of the Martyrs, the prayers and penances of the Saints, the good deeds of all the faithful, take part in that work which, nevertheless, is perfect without them. He saves us by His blood, but it is through and with ourselves that He saves us. Dear Lord, teach us to suffer with Thee, make it pleasant to us to suffer for Thy sake, and sanctify all our sufferings by the merits of Thy own.

**Our Father
Hail Mary
Glory Be**

Lord Jesus, crucified, have mercy on us!

STABAT MATER

*Is there one who would not weep
Whelmed in miseries so deep
Christ's dear Mother to Behold?*

Sixth Station ... Veronica wipes the face of Jesus

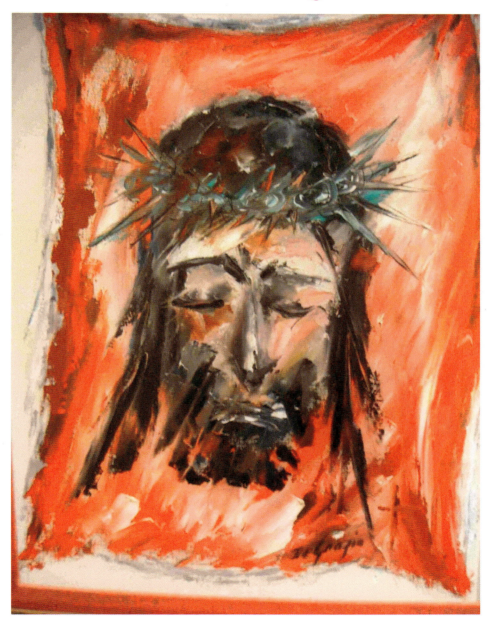

A reading from the second letter of Saint Paul to the Corinthians 4:6

God, who said, "Let light shine out of darkness," has shone in our hearts to give the light of the knowledge of the glory of God in the face of Christ.

A Reading from the Book of Psalms 27:8-9

Of you my heart has spoken: "Seek his face." It is your face, O Lord, that I seek; hide not your face. Dismiss not your servant in anger; you have been my help. Do not abandon or forsake me, O God my help!

A Reading from Isaiah 53: 2-3

*There was in him no stately bearing
to make us look at him,
nor appearance that would attract us to him.
He was spurned and avoided by men,
a man of suffering, accustomed to infirmity,
One of those from whom men hide their faces.*

We adore you O Christ, and we praise you.

Because by your Holy Cross you have redeemed the world.

A Prayer Meditation by Saint Francis of Assisi

Veronica, impelled by devotion and compassion, presents her veil to Jesus to wipe His disfigured face. And Jesus imprints on it His holy countenance: a great recompense for so small a service. What return to you make to your Saviour for His great and manifold benefits?

Most merciful Jesus! What return shall I make for all the benefits Thou hast bestowed upon me? Behold I consecrate myself entirely to Thy service. I offer and consecrate to Thee my heart: imprint on it Thy sacred image, never again to be effaced by sin.

A Prayer Meditation by Blessed John Henry Newman

JESUS let the pious woman carry off an impression of His Sacred Countenance, which was to last to future ages. He did this to remind us all, that His image must ever be impressed on all our hearts. Whoever we are, in whatever part of the earth, in whatever age of the world, Jesus must live in our hearts. We may differ from each other in many things, but in this we must all agree, if we are His true children. We must bear about with us the napkin of St. Veronica; we must ever meditate upon His death and resurrection, we must ever imitate His divine excellence, according to our measure. Lord, let our countenances be ever pleasing in Thy sight, not defiled with sin, but bathed and washed white in Thy precious blood.

Our Father
Hail Mary
Glory Be

Lord Jesus, crucified, have mercy on us!

STABAT MATER

Can the human heart refrain
From partaking in her pain,
In that Mother's pain untold?

Seventh Station ... Jesus falls the second time

A Reading from the Book of Psalms 22:8,12

All who see me deride me. They curl their lips, they toss their heads. Do not leave me alone in my distress; come close, there is none else to help.

A Reading from the Book of Psalms 118:11,12-13,18

They surrounded me ... They surrounded me like bees, they blazed like a fire of thorns; in the name of the Lord I cut them off! I was pushed hard, so that I was falling, but the Lord helped me. The Lord has punished me severely, but he did not give me over to death

A Reading from Lamentations 3: 1-2, 9, 16

*I am a man who knows affliction
from the rod of his anger,
one whom he has led and forced
to walk in darkness, not in the light....
He has blocked my ways with fitted stones,
and turned my paths aside....
He has broken my teeth with gravel,
pressed my face in the dust.*

We adore you O Christ, and we praise you.

Because by your Holy Cross you have redeemed the world.

A Prayer Meditation by Saint Francis of Assisi

The suffering Jesus, under the weight of His cross, again falls to the ground; but the cruel executioners do not permit Him to rest a moment. Pushing and striking Him, they urge Him onward. It is the frequent repetition of our sins which oppress Jesus. Witnessing this, how can I continue to sin?

O Jesus, Son of David, have mercy on me! Offer me Thy helping hand, and aid me, that I may not fall again into my former sins. From this very moment, I will earnestly strive to reform: nevermore will I sin! Thou, O sole support of the weak, by Thy grace, without which I can do nothing, strengthen me to carry out faithfully this my resolution.

A Prayer Meditation by Blessed John Henry Newman

SATAN had a second fall, when our Lord came upon earth. By that time he had usurped the dominion of the whole world—and he called himself its king. And he dared to take up the Holy Saviour in his arms, and show Him all kingdoms, and blasphemously promise to give them to Him, His Maker, if He would adore him. Jesus answered, "Begone, Satan!"—and Satan fell down from the high mountain. And Jesus bare witness to it when He said, "I saw Satan, as lightning, falling from heaven." The Evil One remembered this second defeat, and so now he smote down the Innocent Lord a second time, now that he had Him in his power. O dear Lord, teach us to suffer with Thee, and not be afraid of Satan's buffetings, when they come on us from resisting him.

Our Father
Hail Mary
Glory Be

Lord Jesus, crucified, have mercy on us!

STABAT MATER

Bruised, derided, cursed, defiled,
She beheld her tender child,
All with bloody scourges rent.

Eighth Station ... Jesus meets the women of Jerusalem

A Reading from the Holy Gospel according to Luke 23:27-32

There followed him a great multitude of the people, and of women who bewailed and lamented him. But Jesus turning to them said, "Daughters of Jerusalem, do not weep for me, but weep for yourselves and for your children.

For behold, the days are coming when they will say, 'Blessed are the barren, and the wombs that never bore, and the breasts that never gave suck!' Then they will begin to say to the mountains, 'Fall on us'; and to the hills, 'Cover us.' For if they do this when the wood is green, what will happen when it is dry?"

We adore you O Christ, and we praise you.

Because by your Holy Cross you have redeemed the world.

A Prayer Meditation by Saint Francis of Assisi

These devoted women, moved by compassion, weep over the suffering Savior. But He turns to them, saying: "Weep not for Me, Who am innocent, but weep for yourselves and for your children." Weep thou also, for there is nothing more pleasing to Our Lord and nothing more profitable for thyself, than tears shed from contrition for thy sins.

O Jesus, Who shall give to my eyes a torrent of tears, that day and night I may weep for my sins? I beseech Thee, through Thy bitter and bloody tears, to move my heart by Thy divine grace, so that from my eyes tears may flow abundantly, and that I may weep all my days over Thy sufferings, and still more over their cause, my sins.

A Prayer Meditation by Blessed John Henry Newman

EVER since the prophecy of old time, that the Saviour of man was to be born of a woman of the stock of Abraham, the Jewish women had desired to bear Him. Yet, now that He was really come, how different, as the Gospel tells us, was the event from what they had expected. He said to them "that the days were coming when they should say, Blessed are the barren, and the wombs that have not borne, and the breasts which have not given suck." Ah, Lord, we know not what is good for us, and what is bad. We cannot foretell the future, nor do we know, when Thou comest to visit us, in what form Thou wilt come. And therefore we leave it all to Thee. Do Thou Thy good pleasure to us and in us. Let us ever look at Thee, and do Thou look upon us, and give us the grace of Thy bitter Cross and Passion, and console us in Thy own way and at Thy own time.

Our Father
Hail Mary
Glory Be

Lord Jesus, crucified, have mercy on us!

STABAT MATER

For the sins of His own nation
Saw Him hang in desolation
Till His Spirit forth He sent.

Ninth Station ... Jesus falls the third time

A Reading from the second letter of Saint Paul to the Corinthians 5:19–21

In Christ God was reconciling the world to himself, not counting their trespasses against them, and entrusting to us the message of reconciliation; ... We beseech you on behalf of Christ, be reconciled to God. For our sake he made him to be sin who knew no sin, so that in him we might become the righteousness of God.

A Reading from the letter of Saint Paul to the Romans 8:35,37

Who will separate us from the love of Christ? Will hardship, or distress, or persecution, or famine, or nakedness, or peril, or sword?... No, in all these things we are more than conquerors through him who loved us!

We adore you O Christ, and we praise you.

Because by your Holy Cross you have redeemed the world.

A Prayer Meditation by Saint Francis of Assisi

Jesus, arriving exhausted at the foot of Calvary, falls for the third time to the ground. His love for us, however, is not diminished, not extinguished. What a fearfully oppressive burden our sins must be to cause Jesus to fall so often! Had He, however, not taken them upon Himself, they would have plunged us into the abyss of Hell.

Most merciful Jesus, I return Thee infinite tanks for not permitting me to continue in sin and to fall, as I have so often deserved, into the depths of Hell. Enkindle in me an earnest desire of amendment; let me never again relapse, but vouchsafe me the grace to persevere in penance to the end of my life.

A Prayer Meditation by Blessed John Henry Newman

SATAN will have a third and final fall at the end of the world, when he will be shut up for good in the everlasting fiery prison. He knew this was to be his end—he has no hope, but despair only. He knew that no suffering which he could at that moment inflict upon the Saviour of men would avail to rescue himself from that inevitable doom. But, in horrible rage and hatred, he determined to insult and torture while he could the great King whose throne is everlasting. Therefore a third time he smote Him down fiercely to the earth. O Jesus, Only-begotten Son of God, the Word Incarnate, we adore with fear and trembling and deep thankfulness Thy awful humiliation, that Thou who art the Highest, should have permitted Thyself, even for one hour, to be the sport and prey of the Evil One.

Our Father
Hail Mary
Glory Be

Lord Jesus, crucified, have mercy on us!

STABAT MATER

O thou Mother! fount of love,
Touch my spirit from above.
Make my heart with thine accord:

Tenth Station ... Jesus is stripped of his garments

A Reading from the Holy Gospel according to John 19:23-24

When the soldiers had crucified Jesus, they took his clothes and divided them into four parts, one for each soldier. They also took his tunic; now the tunic was seamless, woven in one piece from the top. So they said to one another: "Let us not tear it, but cast lots for it to see who will get it". This was to fulfil what the Scripture says: "They divided my clothes among themselves, and for my tunic they cast lots". And that is what the soldiers did.

A Reading from the Book of Psalms 22:19

They divide my clothing among them, they cast lots for my robe.

We adore you O Christ, and we praise you.

Because by your Holy Cross you have redeemed the world.

A Prayer Meditation by Saint Francis of Assisi

When Our Savior had arrived on Calvary, He was cruelly despoiled of His garments. How painful this must have been because they adhered to His wounded and torn body, and with them parts of His bloody skin were removed! All the wounds of Jesus were renewed. Jesus was despoiled of His garments that He might die possessed of nothing; how happy will I also die after laying aside my former self with all evil desires and sinful inclinations!

Induce me, O Jesus, to lay aside my former self and to be renewed according to Thy will and desire. i will not spare myself, however painful this should be for me: despoiled of things temporal, of my own will, I desire to die, in order to live for Thee

A Prayer Meditation by Blessed John Henry Newman

JESUS would give up everything of this world, before He left it. He exercised the most perfect poverty. When He left the Holy House of Nazareth, and went out to preach, He had not where to lay His head. He lived on the poorest food, and on what was given to Him by those who loved and served Him. And therefore He chose a death in which not even His clothes were left to Him. He parted with what seemed most necessary, and even a part of Him, by the law of human nature since the fall. Grant us in like manner, O dear Lord, to care nothing for anything on earth, and to bear the loss of all things, and to endure even shame, reproach, contempt, and mockery, rather than that Thou shalt be ashamed of us at the last day.

Our Father
Hail Mary
Glory Be

Lord Jesus, crucified, have mercy on us!

STABAT MATER

Make me feel as thou hast felt;
Make my soul to glow and melt
With the love of Christ, my Lord.

Eleventh Station ... Jesus is nailed to the cross

A reading from the Holy Gospel according to John 19:18-22

There they crucified him, and with him two others, one on either side, and Jesus between them. Pilate also wrote a title and put it on the cross; it read, "Jesus of Nazareth, the King of the Jews." Many of the Jews read this title, for the place where Jesus was crucified was near the city; and it was written in Hebrew, in Latin, and in Greek. The chief priests of the Jews then said to Pilate, "Do not write, 'The King of the Jews,' but 'This man said, I am King of the Jews.'" Pilate answered, "What I have written I have written."

A reading From the Holy Gospel according to Mark 15:24-28

And they crucified him, and divided his clothes among them, casting lots to decide what each should take. It was nine o'clock in the morning when they crucified him. The inscription of the charge against him read: "The King of the Jews". And with him they crucified two thieves, one on his right and one on his left. And the Scripture was fulfilled that says: "And he was counted among the lawless"

A Reading from the Holy Gospel according to John 19:23-24

When the soldiers had crucified Jesus, they took his clothes and divided them into four parts, one for each soldier. They also took his tunic; now the tunic was seamless, woven in one piece from the top. So they said to one another: "Let us not tear it, but cast lots for it to see who will get it". This was to fulfil what the Scripture says: "They divided my clothes among themselves, and for my tunic they cast lots". And that is what the soldiers did.

A Reading from the Holy Gospel according to Luke 23: 32-43

Two other men, both criminals, were also led out with him to be executed. When they came to the place called the Skull, they crucified him there, along with the criminals—one on his right, the other on his left. Jesus said, "Father, forgive them, for they do not know what they are doing." And they divided up his clothes by casting lots.

The people stood watching, and the rulers even sneered at him. They said, "He saved others; let him save himself if he is God's Messiah, the Chosen One."

The soldiers also came up and mocked him. They offered him wine vinegar 37and said, "If you are the king of the Jews, save yourself."

There was a written notice above him, which read: this is the King of the Jews.

One of the criminals who hung there hurled insults at him: "Aren't you the Messiah? Save yourself and us!"

But the other criminal rebuked him. "Don't you fear God," he said, "since you are under the same sentence? We are punished justly, for we are getting what our deeds deserve. But this man has done nothing wrong."

Then he said, "Jesus, remember me when you come into your kingdom. "

Jesus answered him, "Truly I tell you, today you will be with me in paradise."

A reading from the Holy Gospel according to John 19:25-27

Standing by the cross of Jesus were his mother, and his mother's sister, Mary the wife of Clopas, and Mary Magdalene. When Jesus saw his mother, and the disciple whom he loved standing near, he said to his mother, "Woman, behold, your son!" Then he said to the disciple, "Behold, your mother!" And from that hour the disciple took her to his own home.

We adore you O Christ, and we praise you.

Because by your Holy Cross you have redeemed the world.

A Prayer Meditation by Saint Francis of Assisi

Jesus, being stripped of His garments, was violently thrown upon the cross and His hands and feet nailed thereto. In such excruciating pains He remained silent, because it pleased His heavenly Father. He suffered patiently, because He suffered for me. How do I act in sufferings and in troubles? How fretful and impatient, how full of complaints I am!

O Jesus, gracious Lamb of God, I renounce forever my impatience. Crucify, O Lord, my flesh and its concupiscence; scourge, scathe, and punish me in this world, do but spare me in the next. I commit my destiny to Thee, resigning myself to Thy holy will: may it be done in all things!

A Prayer Meditation by Blessed John Henry Newman

JESUS is pierced through each hand and each foot with a sharp nail. His eyes are dimmed with blood, and are closed by the swollen lids and livid brows which the blows of His executioners have caused. His mouth is filled with vinegar and gall. His head is encircled by the sharp thorns. His heart is pierced with the spear. Thus, all His senses are mortified and crucified, that He may make atonement for every kind of human sin. O Jesus, mortify and crucify us with Thee. Let us never sin by hand or foot, by eyes or mouth, or by head or heart. Let all our senses be a sacrifice to Thee; let every member sing Thy praise. Let the sacred blood which flowed from Thy five wounds anoint us with such sanctifying grace that we may die to the world, and live only to Thee.

Our Father
Hail Mary
Glory Be

Lord Jesus, crucified, have mercy on us!

STABAT MATER

Holy Mother, pierce me through!
In my heart, each wound renew
Of my Savior crucified.

Twelfth Station ... Jesus dies on the cross

A Reading from the Holy Gospel according to Luke 23:34

"Father, forgive them, for they know not what they do".

A Reading from the Holy Gospel according to John 19: 28-30

After this, when Jesus knew that all was now finished, he said (in order to fulfil the Scripture): "I am thirsty". A jar full of vinegar was standing there. So they put a sponge full of wine on a branch of hyssop and held it to his mouth. When Jesus had received the vinegar, he said: "It is finished". Then he bowed his head and gave up his spirit".

A Reading from the Holy Gospel according to Matthew 27:45-46

Now from the sixth hour there was darkness over all the land until the ninth hour. And about the ninth hour Jesus cried out with a loud voice, "Eli, Eli, lama sabachthani?", that is, "My God, my God, why have you forsaken me?".

We adore you O Christ, and we praise you.

Because by your Holy Cross you have redeemed the world.

A Prayer Meditation by Saint Francis of Assisi

Behold Jesus crucified! Behold His wounds, received for love of you! His whole appearance betokens love: His head is bent to kiss you; His arms are extended to embrace you; His Heart is open to receive you. O superabundance of love, Jesus, the Son of God, dies upon the cross, that man may live and be delivered from everlasting death!

O most amiable Jesus! Who will grant me that I may die for Thee! I will at least endeavor to die to the world. How must I regard the world and its vanities, when I behold Thee hanging on the cross, covered with wounds? O Jesus, receive me into Thy wounded Heart: I belong entirely to Thee; for Thee alone do I desire to live and to die.

A Prayer Meditation by Blessed John Henry Newman

"CONSUMMATUM est." It is completed—it has come to a full end. The mystery of God's love towards us is accomplished. The price is paid, and we are redeemed. The Eternal Father determined not to pardon us without a price, in order to show us especial favour. He condescended to make us valuable to Him. What we buy we put a value on. He might have saved us without a price—by the mere fiat of His will. But to show His love for us He took a price, which, if there was to be a price set upon us at all, if there was any ransom at all to be taken for the guilt of our sins, could be nothing short of the death of His Son in our nature. O my God and Father, Thou hast valued us so much as to pay the highest of all possible prices for our sinful souls—and shall we not love and choose Thee above all things as the one necessary and one only good?

**Our Father
Hail Mary
Glory Be**

Lord Jesus, crucified, have mercy on us!

STABAT MATER

*Let me share with thee His pain,
Who for all our sins was slain,
Who for me in torments died.*

Thirteenth Station ... Jesus is taken down from the cross

A Reading from the Holy Gospel according to John 19: 38

After this Joseph of Arimathea, who was a disciple of Jesus, but secretly, for fear of the Jews, asked Pilate that he might take away the body of Jesus, and Pilate gave him leave. So he came and took away his body.

We adore you O Christ, and we praise you.

Because by your Holy Cross you have redeemed the world.

A Prayer Meditation by Saint Francis of Assisi

Jesus did not descend from the cross but remained on it until He died. And when taken down from it, He in death as in life, rested on the bosom of His divine Mother. Persevere in your resolutions of reform and do not part from the cross; he who persevereth to the end shall be saved. Consider, moreover, how pure the heart should be that receives the body and blood of Christ in the Adorable Sacrament of the Altar.

O Lord Jesus, Thy lifeless body, mangled and lacerated, found a worthy resting-place on the bosom of Thy virgin Mother. Have I not often compelled Thee to dwell in my heart, full of sin and impurity as it was? Create in me a new heart, that I may worthily receive Thy most sacred body in Holy Communion, and that Thou mayest remain in me and I in Thee for all eternity.

A Prayer Meditation by Blessed John Henry Newman

HE is Thy property now, O Virgin Mother, once again, for He and the world have met and parted. He went out from Thee to do His Father's work—and He has done and suffered it. Satan and bad men have now no longer any claim upon Him—too long has He been in their arms. Satan took Him up aloft to the high mountain; evil men lifted Him up upon the Cross. He has not been in Thy arms, O Mother of God, since He was a child—but now thou hast a claim upon Him, when the world has done its worst. For thou art the all-favoured, all-blessed, all-gracious Mother of the Highest. We rejoice in this great mystery. He has been hidden in thy womb, He has lain in thy bosom, He has been suckled at thy breasts, He has been carried in thy arms—and now that He is dead, He is placed upon thy lap. Virgin Mother of God, pray for us.

Our Father
Hail Mary
Glory Be

Lord Jesus, crucified, have mercy on us!

STABAT MATER

Let me mingle tears with thee,
Mourning Him who mourned for me,
All the days that I may live.

Fourteenth Station ... Jesus is laid in the tomb

A Reading from the Holy Gospel according to John 19: 41-42

Now in the place where he was crucified there was a garden, and in the garden a new tomb where no one had ever been laid. So because of the Jewish day of Preparation, as the tomb was close at hand, they laid Jesus there.

A reading from the Holy Gospel according to Matthew 27:57-60

When it was evening, there came a rich man from Arimathea, named Joseph, who also was a disciple of Jesus. He went to Pilate and asked for the body of Jesus. Then Pilate ordered it to be given to him. And Joseph took the body, and wrapped it in a clean linen shroud, and laid it in his own new tomb, which he had hewn in the rock; and he rolled a great stone to the door of the tomb, and departed.

We adore you O Christ, and we praise you.

Because by your Holy Cross you have redeemed the world.

A Prayer Meditation by Saint Francis of Assisi

The body of Jesus is interred in a stranger's sepulcre. He who in this world had not whereupon to rest His head, would not even have a grave of His own, because He was not from this world. You, who are so attached to the world, henceforth despise it, that you may not perish with it.

O Jesus, Thou hast set me apart from the world; what, then, shall I seek therein? Thou hast created me for Heaven; what, then, have I to do with the world? Depart from me, deceitful world, with thy vanities! Henceforth i will follow the Way of the Cross traced out for me by my Redeemer, and journey onward to my heavenly home, there to dwell forever and ever.

A Prayer Meditation by Blessed John Henry Newman

JESUS, when He was nearest to His everlasting triumph, seemed to be farthest from triumphing. When He was nearest upon entering upon His kingdom, and exercising all power in heaven and earth, He was lying dead in a cave of the rock. He was wrapped round in burying-clothes, and confined within a sepulcre of stone, where He was soon to have a glorified spiritual body, which could penetrate all substances, go to and fro quicker than thought, and was about to ascend on high. Make us to trust in thee, O Jesus, that Thou wilt display in us a similar providence. Make us sure, O Lord, that the greater is our distress, the nearer we are to Thee. The more men scorn us, the more Thou dost honour us. The more men insult over us, the higher Thou wilt exalt us. The more they forget us, the more Thou dost keep us in mind. The more they abandon us, the closer Thou wilt bring us to Thyself.

Our Father
Hail Mary
Glory Be

Lord Jesus, crucified, have mercy on us!

STABAT MATER

By the cross with thee to stay,
There with thee to weep and pray,
Is all I ask of thee to give.

The Artists

Ecce Homo ... Lovis Corinth *(1858-1925)*

1 - *Jesus is condemned to death* ... Michelangelo da Caravaggio *(1571-1610)*

2 - *Jesus carries his cross* ... Peter Howson *(born 1958)*

3 - *Jesus falls for the first time* ... Michael Leopold Lucas Willmann *(1630-1706)*

4 - *Jesus meets his afflicted mother* ... Yvonne Cleaver *(active since 1980s)*

5 - *Simon helps Jesus carry his cross* ... Tiziano Vecellio (Titian) *(1490-1576)*

6 - *Veronica wipes the face of Jesus* ... Ettore De Grazia *(1909-1982)*

7 - *Jesus falls the second time* ... Frank Brangwyn *(1867-1956)*

8 - *Jesus meets the women of Jerusalem* ... Peter Howson *(born 1958)*

9 - *Jesus falls a third time* ... Eric Gill *(1882-1940)*

10 - *Jesus is stripped of his garments* ... James Jacques Tissot *(1836-1902)*

11 - *Jesus is nailed to the cross* ... Audrey Frank Anastasi *(active since 1980s)*

12 - *Jesus dies on the cross* ... Matthias Grünewald *(1470-1528)*

13 - *Jesus is taken down from the cross* ... Duccio di Buoninsegna *(c 1255-1320)*

14 - *Jesus is laid in the tomb* ... Gustave Doré *(1832-1883)*

Printed in Great Britain
by Amazon.co.uk, Ltd.,
Marston Gate.